Plymouth's Historic Hoe

Arthur L. Clamp

The Hoe from the Air

This panorama of the Hoe shows the extent of this limestone headland hemmed with a rocky foreshore and crowned with Smeaton's Tower. The large open air swimming pool now forms a headland to Plymouth's famous grandstand and the curve of Hoe Road links the Barbican, from the right, to Millbay on the far left.

This version of the book is virtually as originally published.
There are now additional pages at the back providing information about the author.

The republishing project is being managed by Arthur's grandson, Steven Gibson. We aim to find all the research that he was involved in publishing, preserving it for the next generation as part of 'The Clamp Collection'.

AN INTRODUCTION TO THE HOE

This illustrated booklet is designed to act as a guide for visitors to the area and to be a reminder of what was seen and how the Hoe has been developed. The Hoe or "high place" also means "spur of the hill" and accurately describes this limestone ridge of rock which, at its highest point, reaches a little over 100 feet and formerly covered an extensive area from Millbay, to the west, to Lambhay Hill overlooking the Barbican, to the east.

Many large cities in many countries can claim a special point of interest and for Plymouth it is this famous limestone hill or grandstand from which generations of local folk have seen the comings and goings of many famous ships and people. The promenade and formerly the wide open furze hill, was where the citizens of the old town gathered together, often in their thousands, to celebrate a royal occasion, a victory won on the sea or in far off lands. The gathering of many people on this green-sloped hill still continues and it was here that victory was celebrated at the end of the last war and it was also here that thousands of people waited to welcome the return of Francis Chichester in the dark of early night when he landed at West Hoe Pier in 1967. No doubt this tradition will continue and this famous open area be a focal point in the minds of people to come.

The Hoe has seen many changes and for hundreds of years it was simply an open area of rough grass with few buildings standing on it. The present layout of the area was started in the 1880s when the principal monuments were erected and paths and grassed areas laid out and the area generally tidied up.

The main phases in its changes came about first through the erection of defences along the length of the hill during the reign of Henry VIII, the cutting of two large figures in the turf, known as Gog and Magog, the building of the Royal Citadel in the 1660s which obliterated these figures and covered about thirty-three acres of land and then the laying out of the area more or less in its present form during the 1880s and 1890s.

The most famous episode in the Hoe's history is probably the game of bowls played by Francis Drake when the Spanish Armada was on its course up the English Channel in 1588. Many other events have taken place here. In 1625 10,000 troops paraded here when King Charles I and his Queen came to view the building of the Citadel. Executions, in one form or another, were performed here and in 1797 three soldiers were put to death in front of thousands of people and troops who had gathered for this gruesome event. In 1815 people came here again to see Napoleon proudly standing on the deck of the ship *Bellerphon* on his way to captivity. Festivals of one kind or another feature regularly in books about the Hoe. In 1832 the passing of the Reform Act was celebrated here, 5,000 children sang here in unison in 1863 on the occasion of the marriage of the Prince of Wales and in 1945 dancing with troops and people was led by Lady Astor when news of the ending of hostilities reached Plymouth.

Various buildings have stood on the Hoe long before the present ones were erected. There was a windmill here for hundreds of years, a camera obscura and in 1581 Drake ordered a "mariner's compass" to be set up which was later replaced by a Trinity obelisk for guiding ships into the old harbour at the Barbican and this itself was replaced by the present Smeaton's tower.

There was also a bandstand here for the entertainment of people and the Hoe had a very large and popular pier which was built in 1884 and destroyed in the air raids of 1941.

The western area of the hill has been quarried for many years and limekilns were in operation here for converting the broken stone into dressing for the land. Ships have been wrecked on the rocky foreshore the most famous of which was probably H.M.S. *Dutton* that hit the rocks below the Citadel in the 1790s.

The full story of the Hoe and the many events that have taken place on it would require a large book to relate in detail. It is hoped that this small publication will satisfy the enquiring minds of most visitors who wish to take away pleasant memories of this part of the large historic maritime port of Plymouth.

Arthur L. Clamp,
203 Elburton Road,
Plymstock, Plymouth, Devon

Looking Westwards

This view from the slopes of the Hoe takes in the almost circular West Hoe Pier, the Grand Parade leading to the houses at Rusty Anchor, the deep narrow channel between Rusty Anchor and Drakes Island, the Island and the Mount Edgcumbe estate in Cornwall. All naval ships entering the leaving H.M. Dockyard Devonport, must pass within yards of this part of the Hoe from which excellent views of ships and sometimes personnel lining them can be had.

Gracious Living

The early nineteenth century Elliott Terrace and The Esplanade form a graceful backcloth to this part of the Hoe. The buildings in the left foreground face the Grand Parade and the Royal Western Yacht Club building on its seaward side. Viscount and Viscountess Astor lived in 3 Elliott Terrace which was later given to the city. The childrens' playground is on part of the Hoe which was quarried for its limestone just prior to the turn of the century.

Looking Eastwards

This view of the Hoe is taken from the path leading to Rusty Anchor and the rocky foreshore. The Naval Memorial and Smeaton's Lighthouse will be easily recognised. The Bull ring not quite so easily recognised but the lady is enjoying this quiet part of the Hoe watching the comings and goings of people and pleasure boats from West Hoe Pier.

Lion's Den and the Cattewater
This view of the eastern foreshore of the Hoe takes in the mens only bathing place with its semi-circular changing building known as the *Lion's Den*. Beyond it is the club house of the Royal Corinthian Yacht Club and slipway both overlooked by the very high walls of the Royal Citadel built in the 1660s. The citadel occupied all this foreshore area up until the 1880s when the present Madeira Road was cut to join Commercial Road running into the Barbican. The Cattewater is in the background.

Summer's Day on the Hoe
Thousands of visitors visit Plymouth every year to enjoy the views over Plymouth Sound and walk around the Hoe and gain some appreciation of the role this area has played in the maritime history of this land. Low tide is here at West Hoe Pier looking towards Smeaton's tower and the much smaller watch tower. A large open air swimming pool on the right of this scene allows visitors and local people to swim in safety at all stages of the tides.

West Hoe Rocky Foreshore
Low tide here reveals part of the rocky foreshore and the various attempts made at making access to the water possible. Hoe Road is buttressed in various places with supporting limestone walls while a small dwelling is actually built on the rocks within feet of the water. The trees in the background are part of the childrens' play area along Pier Street.

Pleasure Boats from the Hoe
Many boats ply for trade from the Barbican round to this foreshore of the Hoe. Visitors are frequently taken up the Hamoaze to see the warships in H.M. Dockyard, Devonport, or higher up the Tamar past Saltash. Some boats will also go down to Looe and Looe Island or along the Devon coast to Newton Ferrers when tides are favourable. Visitors are seen here waiting for a boat coming to moor alongside the small landing stage while two others are moored alongside West Hoe Pier.

Royal Western Yacht Club
The club's flagstaff forms a framework in this view showing the ensign flying in the prevailing south-west wind. This is one of the premier yachting clubs in the area which was formed in 1827. It is closely involved with the planning and running of transatlantic races and welcomed Francis Chichester ashore within a few metres of the building in May, 1967, after he had sailed single-handed from Australia.

Plymouth's Young Fishermen
The West Pier quayside has always been a favourite spot for local anglers whatever age they may be. Here they make up part of the scene on the western side of the Hoe with the tall Naval Memorial in the background. There is good fishing to be had in the Sound especially at the turn of the tide.

1832 Reform Act

Such was the jubilation felt at the passing of this Act that all kinds of local celebrations took place in the Three Towns of Plymouth, Devonport and Stonehouse. 26,000 people met in the nearby Bull Ring to support it. The passing of this glorious Act is now remembered by this stone plaque set in the wall below the Hoe almost opposite the open air swimming pool.

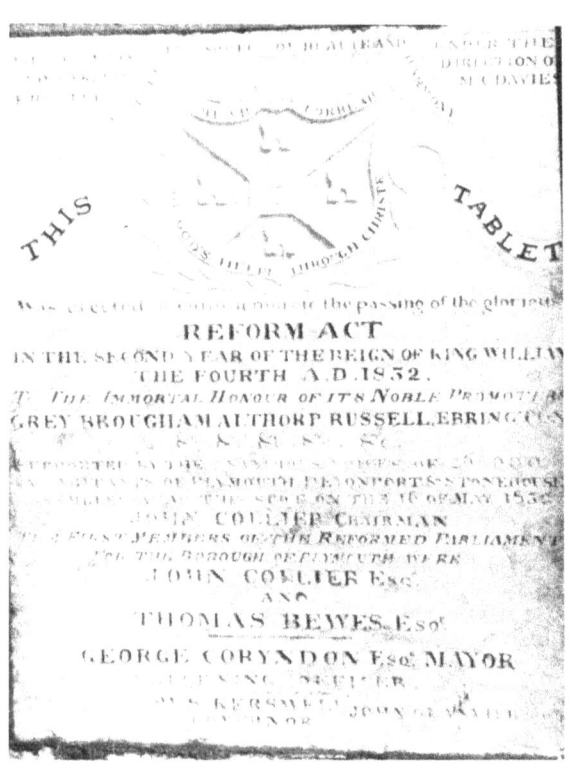

The Belvedere and Bull Ring

This fine three-tiered building was constructed in the early 1890s for people to rest and shelter in when viewing the magnificent sweep of the Sound and to see the comings and goings of naval ships as they pass close to the Hoe sailing to and from H.M. Dockyard, Devonport. A notice on the higher building reads, "Erected 1891-1892 Alderman F. W. Harris, Mayor, Alderman Tho. Pitts, J.P., Chairman of the Hoe Committee." The supporting stone columns are believed to have come from a much earlier building in the old town which was being demolished in the 1870s. The lower part commemorates the almost daily practice of baiting bulls on the Hoe before they were slaughtered to make their flesh tender. Butchers were, in fact, fined for not carrying out this procedure. In 1663 there was paid, *for a great bull rope, for a stake, and unto the smith for baiting of bulls, 16s.* Baiting bulls was banned by Plymouth about 1815.

Pleasure and Leisure

The above view shows part of the western side of the Hoe with the early nineteenth century houses of The Esplanade, Elliott Terrace and Cliff Road. The last is now a large hotel whereas the first two are still used as residences. No 3 Elliott Terrace is now used by the Lord Mayors of the City. It was the home of Lord Astor from 1879 to 1919 and Lady Astor until 1964. She was the first woman Member of Parliament to take her seat in the House of Commons representing Plymouth Sutton ward. The Mayflower Post hotel stands on the left. It is very appropriate that there should be a bowling green on Plymouth Hoe. The public bowling green is close to the Naval Memorial and its club was founded in 1921. Sir Francis Drake's famous game of bowls was not played here. It is thought that he played either on ground where the citadel is or on one of the many greens provided by the old inns which once offered fare around the Hoe.

The Eight-sided Tower

Seven sides with recessed windows and one side for a door form this small structure surmounted with a castellated rim. It overlooks the Hoe Road and large open air swimming pool and observers could look in almost all directions while waiting for the sighting of a mail steamer coming up the English Channel. The shelter was necessary during the wet and often cold winter days.

Victorian Watch Tower

This quaint little limestone building was erected in the 1870s for the benefit of firms waiting for the arrival of transatlantic mail steamers to Plymouth. For about fifty years the port was the first call for these large ships from which passengers use to disembark to catch fast trains to London from Millbay with the mail. Subscribers could also use this tower to learn of new arrivals as quickly as possible. It was later used as a police and ambulance call point but is now empty.

The Green Slopes of the Hoe

The slopes and pathways provide many a visitor with a good excuse to exercise themselves and then to rest on one of the many seats or grass. The lookout or watch tower is the centre piece here below which winds Hoe Road cut in 1817. The arm of Mount Batten breakwater is in the middle distance built in the 1880s.

Swimming off the Hoe

Although the Hoe cannot boast of any good stretches of sand there are many safe spots for swimming reached by steps built by the city fathers over the rocks. Many local families come here for the day enjoying swimming in the clear water and then sunning themselves on the rocks.

Smeaton's Tower

This was the third lighthouse to stand on the Eddystone reef fourteen miles out from land. It warned shipping of the dangerous waters of that area and the many rocks hidden below the water line. The first lighthouse lasted from 1698 to 1703 and was made of wood. It was blown down in a severe gale with its builder, Henry Winstanley, who had stated that it could withstand any tempestuous conditions. The second light was constructed with stone and wooden cladding by John Rudyerd and it burnt down in 1755 having been erected in 1706.

John Smeaton's light was working from 1759 to 1877 when most of it was taken down and re-erected on the Hoe. The rock on which it had stood was being undermined by the sea of which the stump can still be seen on a clear day standing close to the present lighthouse. This was built by James Douglas in 1882. Keepers maintained the houses until 1982 when their services were withdrawn.

Unmanned Eddystone Light

This plaque records the centenary of the erection of Smeaton's tower on the Hoe and the withdrawal of lighthouse keepers from the Eddystone in 1982. Modern lighthouse maintenance techniques enable the light to be controlled from the land with occasional inspections taking place through the use of helicopters.

Ark Royal Anchor

This very large anchor stands in Armada Way by Notte Street. The inscription reads, "This Anchor from H.M.S. *Ark Royal* was presented to the Lord Mayor Councillor Graham Jinks, for The City of Plymouth by Admiral of the Fleet the Lord Hill-Norton, G.C.B., on behalf of the Admiralty Board on 24th April, 1980."

Naval War Memorial

The post-war planning of the city centre enables this large memorial to be seen across the heart of Plymouth from Armada Way. It was erected after the First World War to commemorate all the sailors lost and now includes those who gave their lives during the Second World War. The tall obelisk has four buttresses at its corners with lions and around its base are numerous panels listing those who have fallen in the various theatres of war. There are two bronze groups of sea horses, one with Neptune and the other with Amphitrite, at the entrance to the sunken gardens. There is an alphabetical list of 7,268 names covering 1914-18 and 15,175 names for 1939-45 in the central library, Tavistock Road, which can be seen by the public.

Dedicatory Panels

This is one of four panels fixed to the memorial giving details of the various actions in the wars and the many overseas contingents who supported England during those troubled times. Smaller panels, as seen above, no doubt will bring back memories of those harsh days where dates are given for different engagements. A large service is always held here on Remembrance Day with many representatives of the city and the Navy in attendance.

Smeaton Tower Views

These three were taken from the top of the tower. This one clearly shows part of the extent of the very thick citadel wall with cannon still in position although never used. The Royal Marine statue forms a centre point on the small grassed area over which looks the offices and laboratories of the Marine Biological Association opened in 1888. The public aquarium is housed in the outer building.

Armada Way

This broad vista passes through the heart of the rebuilt city centre providing an excellent view of the Hoe from its northern end. The Naval Memorial is in the foreground behind which stands the civic building opened by H.M. The Queen in 1962. The prominent building on the right is the Holiday Inn and the conference centre only a matter of metres away from the Hoe's grassy slopes. Armada Way is well worth walking from end to end to gain a good understanding of the extent of the post-war rebuilding plan.

Madeira Road

This links the Hoe to the Barbican and follows the rocky foreshore round past Fisher's Nose and Phoenix Wharf where it joins Commercial Road. It was cut in the 1880s through land then occupied by the citadel which had access right down to the water's edge. Part of the outworks of the citadel now stand separate to the main building at Fisher's Nose. The citadel used to have its own quay below the road where the rocks have been cut away.

Drake's Plaque
This is on a house at the top of Looe Street and was originally thought to have been one of many town properties he bought after his successful expeditions. It is now considered that he did not live here but occupied a house closer to the old harbour.

Exploits of Drake
He lived from the 1540s to the 1590s and packed into this span an almost unending round of adventurous, even dangerous, exploits covering much of the New World and, of course, achieving the distinction of circumnavigating the world, crossing many unchartered waters. He married a local girl, Mary Newman, at St. Budeaux in 1569 and, in 1585, married Elizabeth Sydenham after Mary's death.

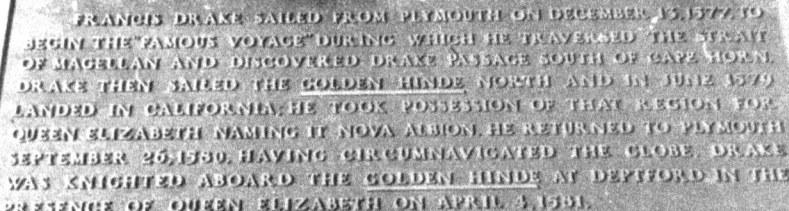

Drake's Statue
This very fine statue facing Plymouth Sound and the Promenade is matched with the nearby statue commemorating the defeat of the Spanish Armada in 1588. Drake was born near Tavistock and a statue stands in that town upon which this one is based. It was designed by the sculptor, Boehm, and was unveiled by Lady Elliot Drake in 1884. The pedestal is of Aberdeen granite. Drake was Member of Parliament for Plymouth in 1584, was largely responsible for bringing water into the small town (Drake's leat) and St. Nicholas Island in the Sound was renamed Drake's Island. The plaque on the left was placed here in 1977 recording his famous circumnavigation which was just one of many of his exploits.

Triple Execution

This cross, set in the pathway near the Naval Memorial, shows the position where three soldiers were shot in 1797 for their part in a mutiny. It was recorded that thousands of people and troops from the citadel assembled on the Hoe to witness the event. There have been many hangings and executions on this open land which, fortunately, had stopped by 1800.

The Armada Statue

"Armada" is a Spanish word meaning "armed force" and this well described the very large fleet which sailed up the English Channel in 1588 to attack and land troops in England. News of the fleet's approach reached Drake while he was playing the now famous game of bowls on the Hoe. Aware of the prevailing south-west wind which aided the Spanish fleet, he waited and in due time left Sutton Harbour and the Cattewater to sail up behind the Armada which was successfully attacked off Portland Bill and Calais. The Spanish fleet was made up of about 130 ships, manned by over 7,000 sailors, and carried about 17,000 troops. It had about 2,000 cannon in readiness and was stocked with food to last six months. This fitting memorial to Drake's brilliant achievement now reminds visitors of the changing fortunes of this country through this defeat and the determination of Drake in breaking the hold the Spanish ships had over the seas of the New World.

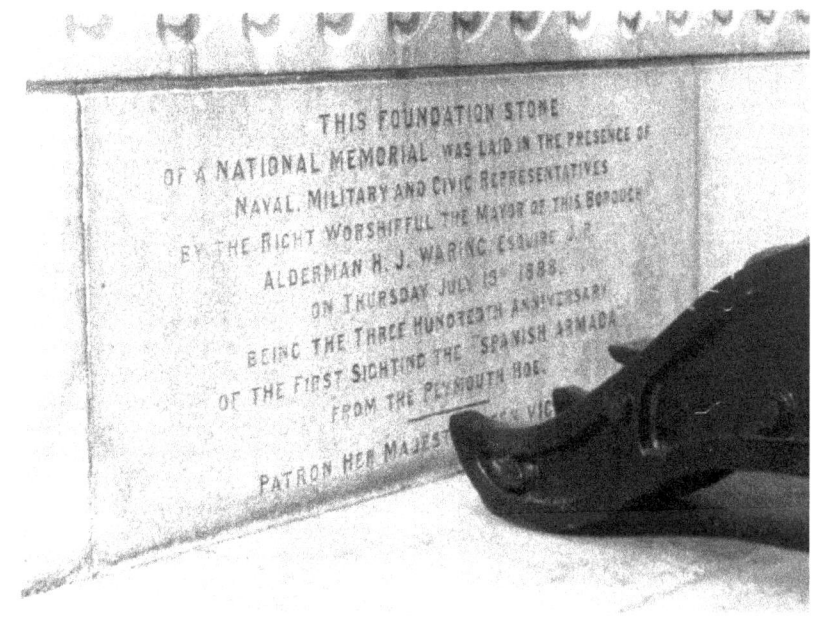

Hoe Garden

This small ornamental garden at the eastern end of the promenade was laid out as part of a scheme for making the Hoe more accessible to the public and to tidy up the area. It is always a great pleasure to visitors and Plymothians to see the splendour of the flowers and the never ending show of colour attained through the skill of the city gardeners. The clock replaces an ornamental water fountain at the base of which reads, "Prejoma Clock presented by Preston John Ball in memory of his parents John and Mary Ball 1965."

Hoe Lodge

This elegant residence was built when the promenade and paths were laid out in the 1880s. The head gardener for the Hoe and parks of the old town lived in it. It is still occupied by a member of the Parks Department of the city and is always surrounded by well kept gardens. The plaque on its east side reads, "Erected 1887-8 during the Mayoralities of W. H. Alger, Esq., and H. J. Warring, Esq. T. Pitts, Esq., Chairman of the Committee." The old crest of the town stands out above the lettering.

Boer War Memorial

This stands near the Citadel and was unveiled by Lady Buller in 1903. Four metal plaques depict engagements at Ladysmith and other places and record that Alfred Mosely erected the obelisk in the memory of Prince Schleswig-Holstein and officers and men who fell during the war from 1899 to 1902. One plaque records, "One point in our position was occupied by the enemy the whole day but at dusk in a very heavy rainstorm they were turned out of the position at the point of the bayonet in the most gallant manner by the Devon Regiment led by Colonel Park."

Public Water Fountain

This stands on the north side of the Hoe and was given to Plymouth by C. Norrington of Tavistock. It had four drinking cups and basins but they are now damaged. Its plaque reads, "Presented to the town of Plymouth by Charles Norrington of Abbotsfield in memory of his wife Marianne Norrington 1881. Thirsty and you gave us drink."

Royal Citadel's West Sally Port

The Arms of King Charles the Second and a crown grace this former gateway into the citadel allowing its troops easy access to the Hoe for parades and marching. It has been sealed up for some years but can still be closely examined from Hoe Road opposite the incline to the Hoe itself.

Royal Marines Statue

This very fine statue commemorates those Marines who fell in the two world wars. On one side it reads, "Erected by the Plymouth Division Royal Marines (past and present) to the Memory of their comrades who fell in the Great War 1914-1919, 1939-1945." The south face reads, "So he passed over and all the trumpets sounded for him on the other side."

The Royal Citadel upon the Hoe

These four photographs show just a small part of this very large seventeenth century military fortification which is still occupied by troops. It is used by the Royal Artillery and was built during the 1660s and originally surrounded on its landward side by a moat. The impressive gateway opens onto a very large central parade ground which is overlooked by various guns and cannon. Visitors are admitted but must accompany the guide at specified times. The walk around the high walls give excellent views over the Hoe, Sound and entrance to Sutton Harbour. The chapel of St. Katherines within the citadel is also open to visitors which has a very interesting interior.

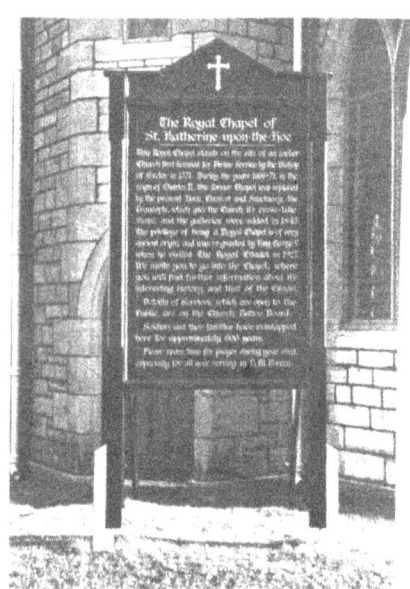

Plymouth's Historic Barbican

Arthur L. Clamp

A Wall of New Plaques

These are on the wall just above the former boatmens' shelter overlooking the Mayflower Stone and record old and new events such as the sailings of the two transport ships carrying convicts to Australia in 1788 and the emigration of Cornish people in the last century to the same country. Other plaques record tragedies of recent times.

AN INTRODUCTION TO HISTORIC BARBICAN

It was in this area that Plymouth first grew from a small settlement surrounding the very old Sutton Harbour under the lee of the Hoe and out of sight of marauding ships on the lookout for easy pickings along this coast. The very early town spread towards the centre of the present city and was defended by walls and earthworks along the Hoe with a castle overlooking the entrance to the harbour on Lambhay Hill. Known as the Barbican or outer defence of the castle, it referred to the land and waterside which came under the protection of the small fort.

The present general appearance of this part of Plymouth which fortunately was spared the widespread damage of the shopping area during the last war, dates from the very prosperous years of the Elizabethan era when the English navy had command over much of the sea. Many of the streets and buildings go back to the 1500s and 1600s when the harbour and nearby Cattewater were the main berthing areas of the English fleet.

The actual quaysides and the layout of the waterfront date much later when various schemes were undertaken to extend the original quays and provide better and larger berthing facilities for larger vessels. The former fish market, Quay Road and much of the Sutton Harbour frontage date from the last century. The piers to the old entrance to the harbour were built in the 1790s.

Many changes have taken place in this rather small area through the fortunes and misfortunes of war, trade and the opening up of new and exciting lands overseas. The secure harbour was often the last port of call for ships making their way to the New World. Numerous voyages of exploration started from here some of which have been commemorated on the West Pier.

The Barbican became heavily congested with people and buildings during the last century and became run down to such an extent that plans were made for demolishing large portions of it after the last world war. Fortunately through the foresight of some local people many buildings have now been restored and the area developed into its present thriving use mainly for visitors with an enlarged fish market on its far side.

Changes have taken place and most of the old trades and crafts linked with the sea, wine trade, fishing and shipping have been replaced with leisure pursuits and shops now cater mainly for the tourists more than the needs of local people. However, there is still some chandlery facilities here, warehouses partly in use and the now very active new fish market available to boats at all states of the tide.

Most of the points of interest in the Barbican are shown in this booklet and a brief description of them is given. Visitors would do well to leave their cars away from here and explore the waterfront, narrow opes, streets, piers and buildings on foot.

Arthur L. Clamp,
203 Elburton Road,
Plymouth, Devon PL9 8HX

Old Custom House

It was to this small granite building overlooking the Parade that Elizabethan captains and ship owners, including Sir Francis Drake, came to pay dues on imported goods and to record the extensive trade in wine, cloths, etc., handled here up until 1820 when the larger custom house opposite was opened.

The tall narrow wall painting by the Barbican artist, Robert Lenkiewicz, is in Southside Street entitled the *Last Judgement* painted in 1985.

Lambhay Hill

A four-towered castle once controlled the entrance to Sutton Harbour from this hill of which one tower remains. It was part of a line of defences covering the Hoe dating from the fourteenth century. The present arms of Plymouth incorporate the old castle quadrant or towers. Below is the commemorative Australian plaque recalling the contribution made by the R.A.A.F. when stationed at Mount Batten during the Second World War. The engraved stone records the former boatmens' shelter and one of the more recent plaques tells of six vessels leaving Plymouth in the 1840s with settlers for New Zealand.

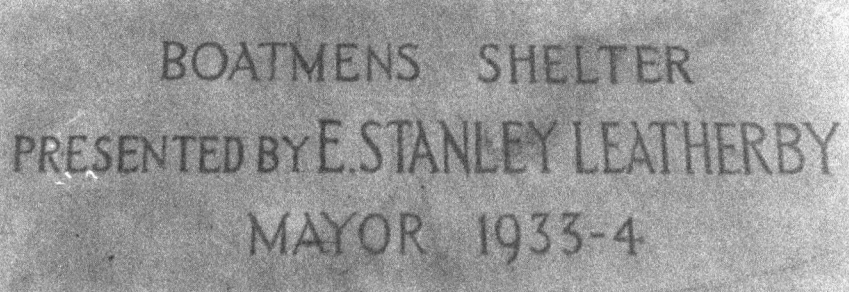

West Pier Commemorative Plaques

This small pier has many plaques and stones recording numerous voyages to and from the old port of Plymouth town. This page shows five of them the two immediately below having been erected in 1962 and 1983. No doubt others will be placed here to add interest to this locality and for visitors. The crown marks the departure of H.M. The Queen and the Duke of Edinburgh from this pier in 1962 and below it is the most recent plaque which recalls the voyage by Sir Humphrey Gilbert that led to the Newfoundland claim in 1583. The return of the Tolpuddle Martyrs is similarly recorded while two stones commemorate the departure of the *Tory* and the *Sea Venture* from here.

Passage to New Zealand
This stone commemorates the departure of the ship *Tory* from Plymouth in March, 1839, on its pioneering voyage to colonise New Zealand.

Admiral Sir John Somer's Flagship, 1609
The *Sea Venture* left Plymouth on 2nd June, 1609, with 150 people on board including Sir Thomas Gates. It was wrecked on a Bermuda reef but ten months later two more vessels were built and the people sailed on to Jamestown. Further details of this voyage are on a plaque next to this stone.

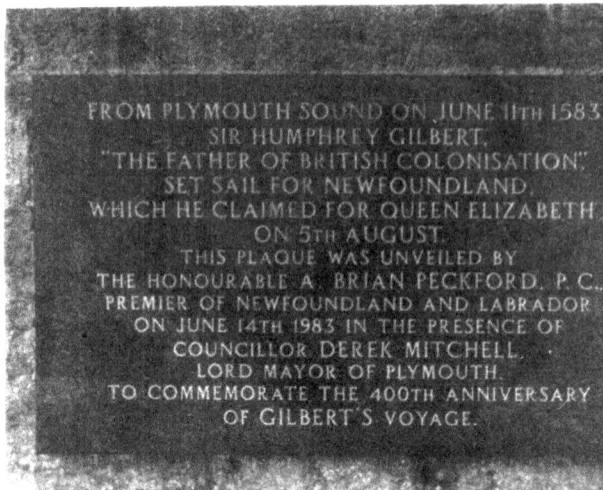

Barbican Glassworks
This was opened in May, 1997, by the Dartington Crystal Company and occupies the old fish market erected in 1891. It has a large display/shop area and a studio where visitors can see glass blowing taking place.

Sutton Harbour Lock Gates
Viewed against Lambhay Hill these gates hold back the water in the harbour and allow boats to enter and leave round the clock. They were opened in November, 1993, and have added significantly to the volume of trade taking place in the new fish market.

Southside Street
This is the main thoroughfare of the Barbican which escaped the heavy blitz of the last world war. It was paved in 1582 and originally fronted the water's edge. The buildings on the left were carefully restored in the 1930s while others are of a much later period some converted into shops catering for visitors. The chimney of the former distillery is the background.

The Navy Inn
This old established Barbican inn is suitably named and now faces a new large glass-fronted neighbour, the Barbican Glassworks which was opened in 1997. The inn almost stood on the edge of the old quay which was extended to carry the former fish market in 1891.

Shipping Yacht Chandler
This is the last of thirteen similar businesses around Southside Street offering a great variety of ropes, fittings, clothing, etc., to the once many mariners working here. Now this shop, set up in 1905 and run by the same family, serves the needs of leisure craft and yacht owners. The *Dolphin Hotel* has met other needs of fishermen and mariners for more years than anyone can remember.

List of Pilgrim Fathers
A large wall board on the Island House lists those who sailed from Plymouth in 1620 to the New World. The details are very interesting as they give the trade and place of work of the passengers none of whom came from Plymouth. The ship had set sail from Southampton calling at Dartmouth and then putting in for repairs at Plymouth.

The Island House
This building stands on its own at the entrance to New Street and probably dates from the years 1590 to 1600 at a time when much of the Barbican was being developed through the prosperity gained by the renowned Elizabethan captains and sailors many of whom lived in this area. The house was first the residence of a wealthy captain then it became a dwelling, a shop and an antique shop It is now an information bureau for visitors. The 1891 alignment of the old quayside is shown by the bollards in the foreground.

Jacka's Bakery in Southside Street
This is one of the oldest bakeries in the country with an oven set in 90 tons of sand dating from the early 1600s. Named after an owner it has only changed hands three times since the turbulent years of the Civil War in the 1640s. A cannon ball was found embedded in a ceiling timber some years back which was thought to have been fired from Mount Batten by the surrounding Royalist forces. Excellent bread and cakes are still made on the premises.

New Street
This was new in the 1580s built with its many fine timbered houses during the prosperous Elizabethan years. Its cobbled surface was familiar to Drake, various members of the Hawkins family, the Pilgrim Fathers and many others who set out from this port to many destinations across the seas. A finely restored merchants house is now open to visitors while other buildings have good carved woodwork on them. The street leads up to the Hoe and the Royal Citadel.

Phoenix Wharf and Fisher's Nose

This part of the Barbican along Commercial Road is now used by many sailing enthusiasts and by pleasure boats taking visitors mainly up the Tamar to see the warships. The road originally only went up as far as the corner at Fisher's Nose until the 1930s although pedestrians could walk through a tunnel in the citadel's walls to reach the Hoe.

Many old buildings stood here until the 1930s used as part of the victualling or food stores for the navy from the middle of the 1600s until the 1830s when the present large Royal William Victualling Yard was built in Stonehouse, Plymouth. From the 1830s to the 1890s about 450,000 people passed through emigration buildings on this waterfront many sponsored by government assisted passages to encourage settlement in North America, Australia and other places. Only the single square building remains from these years.

The Distillery

This large building at the top end of Southside Street has been used for making Plymouth gin and other drinks since 1793. It has been converted into an interesting eating house with a bar. Many artefacts from this long period have been kept making this an unusual and attractive place for visitors. It was used earlier as a debtors' prison and prior to this was described as *a mansion house commonly called the Great House*, then in the ownership of Sir John Hele of Wembury. It was thought that it had links with a monastery but recent research has not substantiated this suggestion.

Southisde Street

This early morning view of its lower end shows the recent traffic calming measures put in place. Leading off from this street are short narrow lanes known as *Opes* going to the quayside or up to the left to the historic New Street. The use of this word is peculiar to the Barbican area and can now be seen in the new decorated lane and street name wall signs.

Entrance to the Great House

This heavy wooden door and granite jambs was the main entrance into the old mansion. The plaque above is wrong and the nearby lane led up to the Grey Friars religious house which was closed in 1538.

Local Fishing Boats
Here is now one of Plymouth's boats which can now land fish at any state of the tide alongside another from Weymouth. The new fish market and around the clock landings have resulted in a great increase in catches being handled here since the recent changes to Sutton Pool and the construction of the lock gates in 1993.

The Old Fish Market
This view of 1911 captures the atmosphere of the former market which was opened in 1891. Half tide prevents the small boats from landing their catches directly into the covered market. The many boats with their sails is what people think of when recalling the old days of Sutton Harbour.

Fish Market
The new and much larger fish market is on the eastern side of Sutton Harbour facing the former one built in 1891 and now converted into a glass centre. The new lock gate enables many more fishing vessels to bring in their catches at all states of the tide. It was opened in July, 1995, and has fully covered facilities for handling the now much larger landings coming in from many parts of the country.

Harvesting the Sea
Many more and larger boats are now able to land catches in Sutton Harbour. Day boats out for twenty-four hours and beamers, out for up to three to six days, land a great variety of fish which can include whiting, red mullet, ponting, plaice, hake, squid, etc. twenty-fours hours a day.

Selling the Fish
Rex Down, Fred Brimacombe and John Taylor look on while a Dover sole is being sold to a local customer in one of the recently opened fish units of the market. Rex Down is holding a wing of a ray, many people come here to buy freshly caught fish in addition to commercial buyers.

Marketing the Harvest of the Sea
Two visitors from Bristol watch the landing of locally caught scallops to be taken by road to North Wales for cleaning then on to Paris for sale in the very large French fish market

Australian Pioneers
Five Plymouth men are recorded on this stone who made their mark on the infant colony so many years ago.

The Custom House and the Parade
This fine five arched building was erected in 1820 to cope with the increasing trade coming into this port. It replaced the much smaller custom house which still stands on the opposite side of the Parade. This part of the Barbican takes its name from the time when Royal Marines used to exercise here in the late 1600s; they were billeted in nearby buildings. The New Quay here was new in the 1570s which was built on reclaimed land and reflected the great prosperity of the Elizabethan years for Plymouth.

Vauxhall Quay and North Quay

This makes up part of the innermost edge of Sutton Harbour and was very busy with commercial traffic up until a few decades ago. *The Three Crowns* inn and a new open area with flats in the background face part of the quay while below the North Quay is now overshadowed with new office and residential blocks with one old limestone warehouse converted in flats. Yachts now berth close by in the Sutton marina reflecting the great change in use of this old trading harbour.

Vauxhall Quay and Warehouses
This small quay built in the 1830s is now overshadowed by the new developments along North Quay. The limestone warehouses were erected in 1822 and have now been coverted into private flats, a trend which has overtaken others in this area. To the left and just out of view is the former offices of A. E. Monsen, ship chandlers, whose office door is adorned by the face of a pirate. To the right stands the new Mariners Court of private flats.

The Cooperage, Sutton Wharf
The title recalls the making of wine and beer barrels by coopers here from 1800. It was one of the many supporting trades taking place around the Barbican serving the needs of ships and the export of goods. It has been put to different uses like many other quayside buildings but retains its very large wooden doors. The wharf was built in the 1810s and railway lines alongside the quayside were laid to Vauxhall Quay in 1879 and used until the 1940s.

Quay Road
This short cobbled quayside road linking the Parade to the old fish market was built on reclaimed land in the 1890s. The large limestone warehouses previously were at the water's edge and, at high tide, sailing vessels could easily moor alongside them and discharge their cargoes by hoist straight into them. The cobbled way is now often used as an outdoor eating area.

Merchants House in St. Andrews Street
This finely restored building is open to the public and dates from the sixteenth century. It was once in the ownership of William Parker, an Elizabethan privateer who raided the Spanish treasure ships in the Carribean in the 1590s. He later became Mayor of Plymouth. Its east front consists of moulded oak framed windows set between limestone walls.

A pole staircase leads up to three floors and the rooms are now used for displaying various items on the history of the city. The house was fully restored in the 1970s having fallen into decay. It now stands in contrast to the surrounding modern buildings.

Bretonside
This takes its name from the burning of the old town by Bretons from France in 1403. The wall plaque records this pillaging act when most of the town was laid waste through fire.

Palace Court
These two local people are attired in the dress of the Pilgrims of 1620 standing in the grounds of the old Palace Court School, High Street. Catherine of Aragon rested here in the former large house after landing from France on her way to London to marry Arthur, Prince of Wales. She brought with her a dowry of 200,000 crowns. A plaque on the wall reads:

> This wall incorporates
> the sole remaining fragments of the
> 15th century building known as
> PALACE COURT
> which stood on this site until its
> demolition in 1880 when the Palace
> School Board was erected.
> The School was reconstructed in 1935,
> destroyed by enemy action in 1941
> and rebuilt in 1951-52.

The Hoe
This view of the Hoe was taken from the high wall of the Royal Citadel and show the large open promenade laid out in the 1880s and various memorials and monuments which have become familiar sights to many visitors to Plymouth.

Note, this content was originally on the front cover of the Barbican booklet, which is why there is space on this page.

The Mayflower Stone

This is one of the most well known of Plymouth's landmarks recording the departure of the Pilgrim Fathers in 1620 from the harbour quayside. Lettering on the bottom reads: The memorial presented by Alderman Sir Frederick Winnicott, J.P. Unveiled by the Right Worshipful The Mayor of Plymouth Councillor Mr. E. Stanley Leatherby on the 5th September, 1934. The United States Consul, Mr. Rollin R. Winslow, who was a direct descendent of one of the Pilgrims, was among many hundreds of people when the stone was unveiled by the dropping of the Union Jack and the Stars and Stripes flags. The portland stone canopy was designed by J. Wibberley, city engineer, in the Doric style and the dated granite block was also moved from its original position to the present site.

The Royal Citadel upon the Hoe, Plymouth

Arthur L. Clamp

An artist's impression of the Royal Citadel.

THE ROYAL CITADEL UPON THE HOE

THIS fortification was built at the order of King Charles II by his chief military engineer, Bernard de Gomme, during the 1660s and has been described as Plymouth's most historic building and one of the finest remaining seventeenth century forts in the country.

It occupies a large area of the eastern end of the Hoe from which its guns could easily defend the entrance to the Cattewater and Sutton Pool then the main berthing areas for the King's Navy. The round tower standing on Mount Batten was part of this defence arrangement and was armed with its own guns.

Plymouth rebelled against the King during the Civil War of the 1640s and it has been said that there was a need for building and arming the fort to cover its landward side. This was to keep a watchful eye on the town's citizens lest their enthusiasm for Parliamentarian causes should break out again.

The citadel stands on the site of the much older Hoe Fort erected about 1590 and the chapel of St. Katherines which replaced an earlier church on the Hoe acting as well as a beacon for ships. The demolition of the very old Hoe Fort started in 1666 the same year that the foundation stone of the citadel was laid by John Grenville, Earl of Bath, and Governor of the town and port of Plymouth. It appears that there were five companies of soldiers on duty during the building of this large fort, the *men handsome and in excellent order wearing red jackets faced with yellow and the Duke of Cornwall's yellow jackets with red linings.* The building was commissioned on 17th November, 1665, although far from complete.

Such was the interest or concern of King Charles II that he came with his brother in 1671 to inspect its progress, then in 1677 by which year it is thought that the citadel was complete. The date 1670 appears on the main entrance gate which may indicate the completion only of that decorated arch.

The building has been described as an irregular bastioned pentagon made of three regular and two irregular bastions linked by curtain walls. In total these are about three quarters of a mile in length part of which can be walked. The ramparts are about seventy feet thick and vary in height from between twenty-five and sixty feet. The various buildings in the chapel are illustrated and described in the following pages.

There was a dry ditch or moat surrounding the fort on its landward sides and there were outer works with a small harbour or landing stage between the main wall and rocky foreshore where Madeira Road runs. The walls are of limestone with granite dressings and the casemates are partly of china stone with the entrances in portland stone. The older parts of the citadel are in a very good state of repair and the much newer buildings inside do not look as though they have been built for many years.

The citadel was originally mounted with 165 guns. Those now on display in the square and on the walls date mainly from the last century and are only of ornamental or historical use. The fort has never been engaged in active fighting. Many cannon were used for practice firing up until 1906 and the buildings have always been occupied by troops and military equipment. The Royal Artillery have been here since about the turn of the century.

Although this very large fort cannot claim to any outstanding military achievement, it has had an interesting number of visitors and some unusual events have taken place in it. By an irony of fate it was constructed with so much care and concern by the Stuarts it played a part in their downfall by being the first fort to surrender to William of Orange when he appeared off the Devon coast with some 500 ships. The Governor, the Earl of Bath, handed over the silver key of the citadel to the Prince of Orange assuring him of his support. The Prince's Declaration was first read in the town's guildhall and then in the citadel concluding with a salute of guns originally mounted some twenty years beforehand to protect the English crown.

The following dates and events are taken from the citadel's records:

1747: A soldier was shot in the citadel for desertion.
1765: A large town fire nearly set alight 123 barrels of gunpowder in the fort.
1779: A spy was caught in the fort but he later bribed his way out.
1789: King George III with Queen Charlotte and his children visited the building.
1796: H.M.S *Dutton* was wrecked below the rocky foreshore of the outer works.
1800: Lord Nelson paid a visit here.
1816: The bodies of Captain R. Kerby and Captain Cooper were found. They were shot for cowardice during action in 1702.
1807: A Spanish treasure ship was brought into Plymouth from which seventeen carts, each hauled by four horses, transferred to safe keeping in the citadel one and a half million silver dollars.
1846: A gun salute welcomed the Royal Yacht with Queen Victoria on board to Plymouth.
1840: Gun firing was recorded from the citadel to a buoy positioned to the right of the breakwater.
1888: Dry ditch filled in and Madeira Road cut below the citadel linking the Barbican with the Hoe.
1927: Approval was given to resume the use of the original title of *The Royal Citadel*.

The building was strongly fortified during both World Wars and it sustained some damage during the 1940s.

Arthur L. Clamp,
203 Elburton Road,
Plymstock, Plymouth.

Field Carriages and Brass Guns

There are four of these close to the parade ground. Two of the guns are light field pieces and two are howitzers all now mounted on later carriages made in 1877. The gun barrels date from the 1850s or 1860s.

Three Guns on Trunnions

The nearest and furthest of these three are sixty-four pounder palliser guns of cast iron with rifled bores dating from 1871. The centre one is also made of cast iron but it has a smooth bore and was made in 1816. The letters w.c.o. refer to the manufacturer, Walker and Company, Rotherham, Yorkshire.

Large Accommodation Block

This very clean cut limestone building facing the parade houses men on duty in the citadel. A stone plaque commemorating the jubilee of Queen Victoria in 1897 is on the wall by one of the doors recording the completion of work on these buildings. An interesting small colannade is on the left wing of this block.

Silver Key to the Citadel

This is the original silver key to the gateway and it is kept in the Officers' Mess in the custody of the officer commanding the Citadel. Whenever officers dine in the mess it is placed on a salver on the table and when members of the Royal family visit here it is always ceremonially presented to them. It is 18 inches long and bears the date 1670 with other dates showing the visit of King Edward VII in 1902, Duke of Connaught in 1917 and King George VI in 1947. King Charles II was presented with the key in 1671.

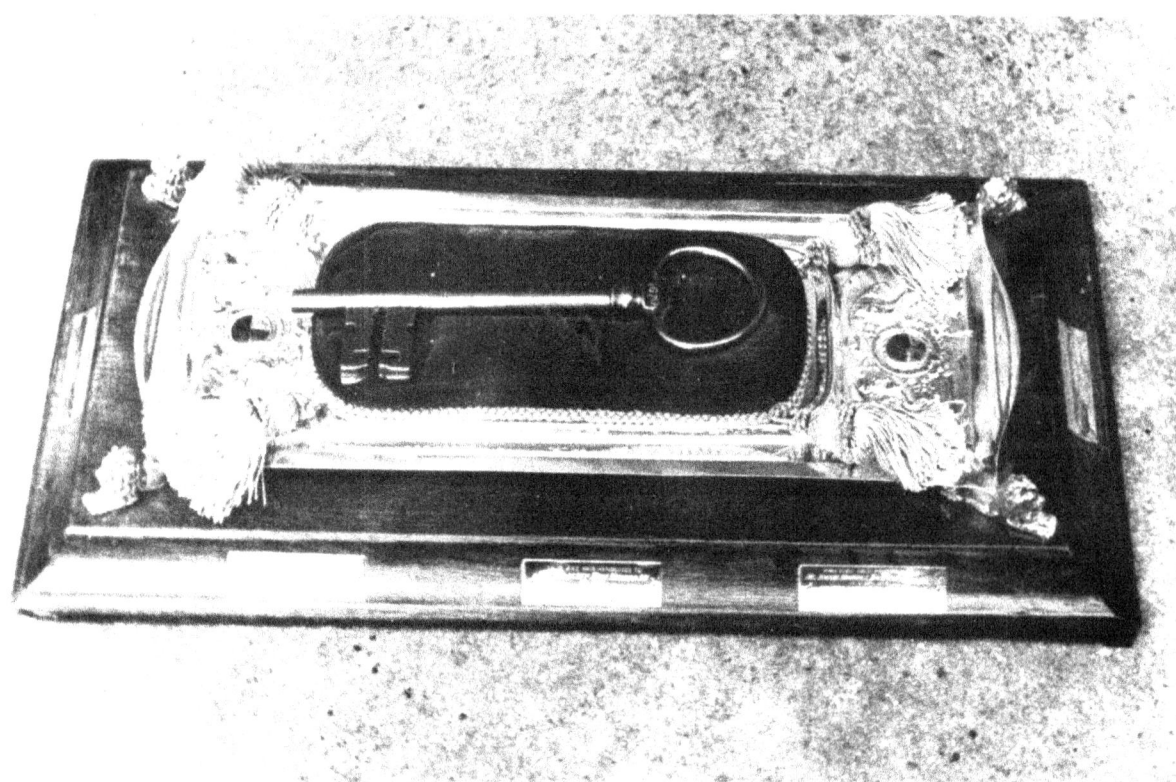

The Governor's House

This fine three storied building faces the parade ground. It was used as an officers' mess during the last century and was converted into offices about 1900. The original door was discovered during alterations which now serves as the main door leading into the present officers' mess. The building is now the Regimental and Quartermaster headquarters.

Ten inch Mortor Gun

Two of these are mounted in front of the above building and were designed for firing from concealed positions for dropping bombs into the enemy at close quarters. Their weight is indicated and they date from the 1840–50s. The letters B.O. on the side refer to the Board of Ordnance which was disbanded in May, 1855, and replaced with the War Department.

Facing the Hoe

Here are two of the citadel's many cannon which overlook the Hoe from the western side of the fortification. These are not the original cannons placed here but date from the last century. Both were made in the foundry of Walker and Company at Rotherham. The upper is an eighteen pounder with the year 1812 marked on it while the lower is a sixty-four pounder made in 1870. Almost all the wall openings or embrasures have cannon in them which give a good idea of what the citadel looked like when it was first fortified.

Facing the Sound

The cannon in these two photographs are perhaps the most well remembered because of their position overlooking the Sound and being seen from outside the Citadel by visitors walking on the Hoe. The four sixty-four pounders are mounted on traversing siege carriages. The gun barrels date from 1870 and are of the palliser construction now positioned with their carriages on restored metal runners.

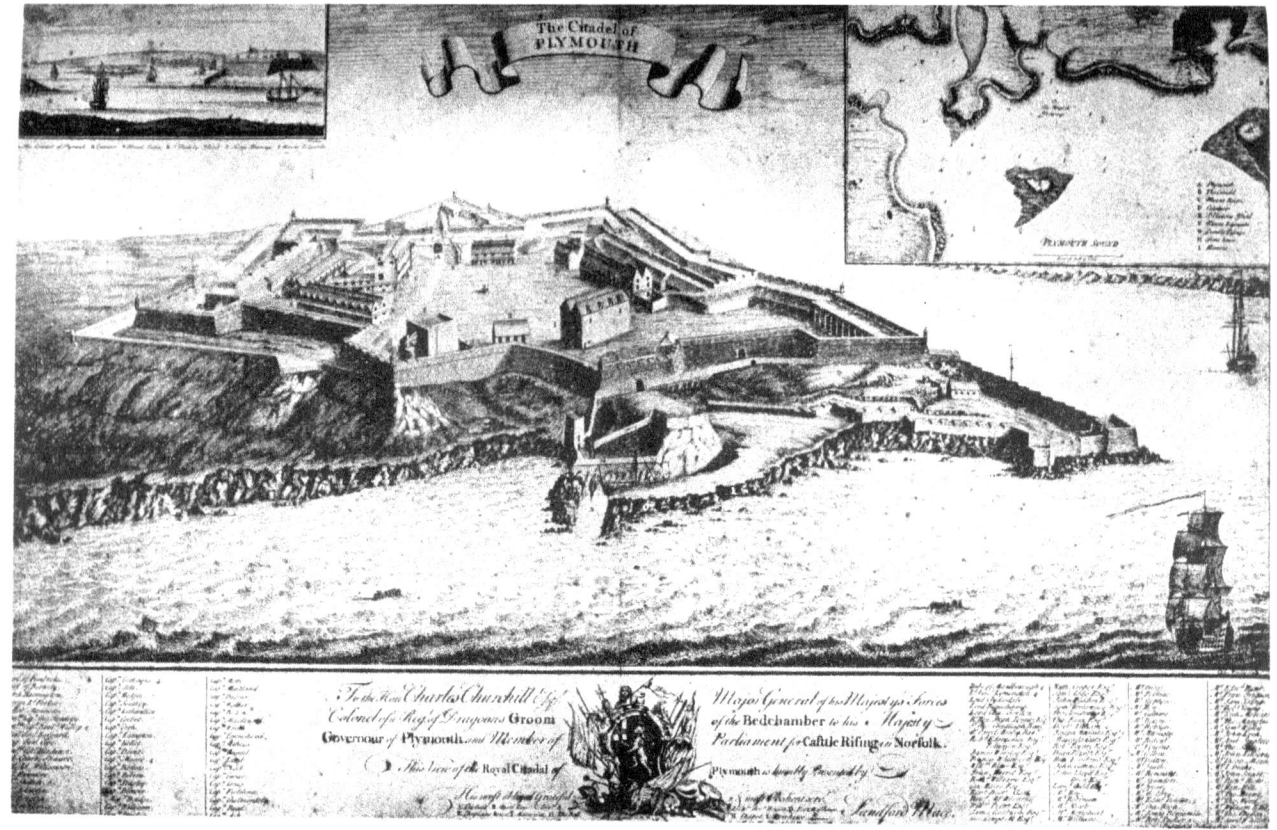

Early Engraving of the Citadel

This 1737 engraving clearly shows the extensive layout of the citadel and the surrounding walls with outworks reaching the rocky foreshore below the main building not then accessible to the public. There was a small harbour cut as part of the original plan.

Soldiers on Duty

Drake's Island, Mt. Edgcumbe, in the distance, and the western area of the Hoe are overlooked in this early nineteenth century engraving of soldiers on duty by the guns on the citadel's high walls. One is holding a swabbing out sponge for cleaning the inside of the barrels. There is also a pile of shot supported by a shot garland next to the wall.

Wreck of H.M.S. Dutton below the Citadel in 1796

This artist's drawing captures the drama of H.M.S. *Dutton*, an east Indian transport ship carrying soldiers and their families of the Queen's Regiment, as she breaks up on the rocks below the citadel. Ropes thrown to the shore enabled many to be saved under the command of Captain Edward Pellow who later received the freedom of Plymouth.

Mount Batten Tower and the Citadel

This engraving views the citadel from Turnchapel with the Mount Batten tower facing the citadel from across the water. It was built at the same time as the citadel and was similarly armed to protect the entrance to the then main harbour of Plymouth.

West Sally Port

This entrance faces the Hoe and was reached by crossing the old dry moat encircling the landward sides of the citadel. The Royal Arms with the decorated letters "C" and "R" can be seen and a well preserved crown stands proud above the now blocked doorway. The west sally port was next in size and architectural finish to the main gate facing north. The use of the word "sally" suggests it was used for soldiers to walk out or march possibly for exercising on the then more open spaces of the Hoe.

Overlooking the Cattewater

This is part of the view from the eastern side of the citadel with Mount Batten and the R.A.F. station across the water and the outworks of the citadel itself overlooking the boat park at Fisher's Nose. Madeira Road, linking the Barbican to the Hoe, was cut during the 1880s separating the main part of the citadel from the rocky foreshore, its old harbour and the building at Fisher's Nose. The Cattewater was for hundreds of years the main harbour for sailing ships in use during Drake's time and later years which was guarded by the guns in the citadel.

King George II Statue

The King is attired as a roman warrior and is crowned with a laurel wreath. The statue was erected by Robert Pitt in 1728 at the expense of Captain Louis du Tour to commemorate the King's ascension to the throne in 1727. It formerly stood in the middle of the square which then comprised of many well kept lawns.

The Old Storehouse

This fine old limestone building faces the square and was originally used as a storehouse for the garrison troops. The main door is blocked but the archway still has the granite side and headstones. The building was converted from a store in 1844. The Royal Arms are a little weather worn and a much later clock now tells the time from an old window recess.

Commemorative Brass Plate

This plate is on the wall of the guardroom and records two years of restoration work on the casemates during the 1840s. These are vaulted arches in the main wall built to hold large guns. It is interesting to read the details on the plate, the work being necessary following a serious fire.

Bell Trophy

Visitors may be surprised to see this gleaming bell hanging outside the army guardroom. It was presented to the 29th Regiment during their tour of Germany in 1954-1956 and comes from a Breman-based ship sunk in the area, the *Sierra Morena*.

The Guardroom and Main Entrance

The rebuilt guardroom is just inside the main entrance to the citadel through which part of the city can be seen in this photograph. The stone work is embellished with the Royal Arms and the structure was intended to form a much larger gatehouse. Access is gained to walk around the top of the wall to the left of the entrance. A little Tudor and Rose gun dating from the 1690s stands between the columns of the guardroom.

Russian Linkhorne Gun of 1824

This gun was captured by the British at the Battle of the Alma in September, 1854, and placed in charge of the Royal Artillery in 1960. This information is on the gun which was housed for many years at Woolwich. It now stands opposite the guardroom and is a poignant reminder of that bitter campaign fought over a hundred years ago. It is a muzzle loading gun and has the date 1831 on it although it was actually made in 1824.

The Garrison Church

St. Katherine upon the Hoe within the Royal Citadel, to give it its full name, was built at the same time as the citadel and replaced a smaller and very much earlier church. This stood on the open Hoe and was used as a beacon for ships as well. St. Katherines has been the garrison church for the various regiments in occupation, its interior displaying many features reflecting this role over the years. The wall plaque below records one incident. The church was enlarged at a later date and is open to the public for Sunday services.

In memory of
GUNNER C. HILL, AND GUNNER F. BETTS,
AGED 30 YEARS. — AGED 21 YEARS.
2 BATTERY 1 BRIGADE SOUTH IRISH DIVISION, R.A,
ACCIDENTALLY DROWNED AT FORT BOVISAND
DURING THE GALE OF 1ST SEPTEMBER 1883,
THIS TABLET IS ERECTED BY THE OFFICERS
N.C, OFFICERS AND MEN OF THE BATTERY.

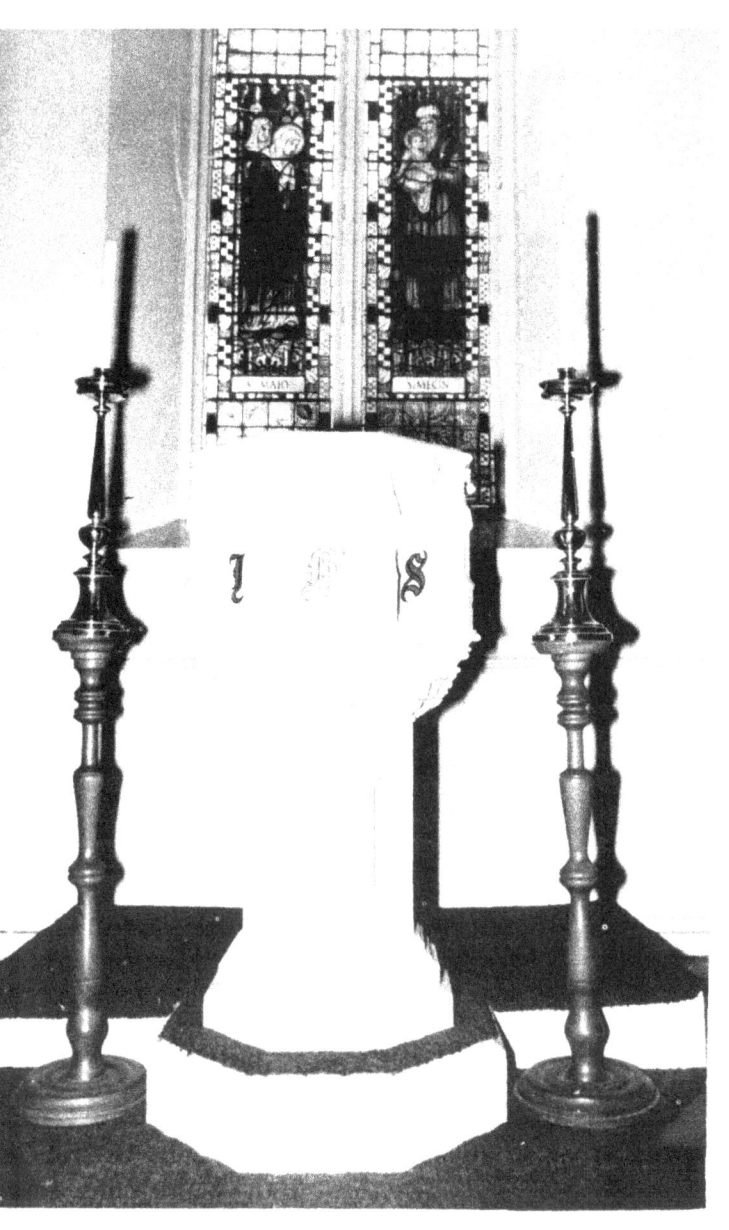

The Font

This was presented by General the Hon. Sir Henry Murray, K.C.B., on 24th May, 1845, following extensive alterations and enlargement to the original building. The stained glass building behind the font came from the damaged garrison church of St. George in Devonport.

The Royal Chapel

This well executed notice board summarises the history of St. Katherines. Many soldiers from different regiments have worshipped here and from 1896 it has been used by the Royal Artillery. The building was damaged during the war and underwent restoration during 1944 and 1946.

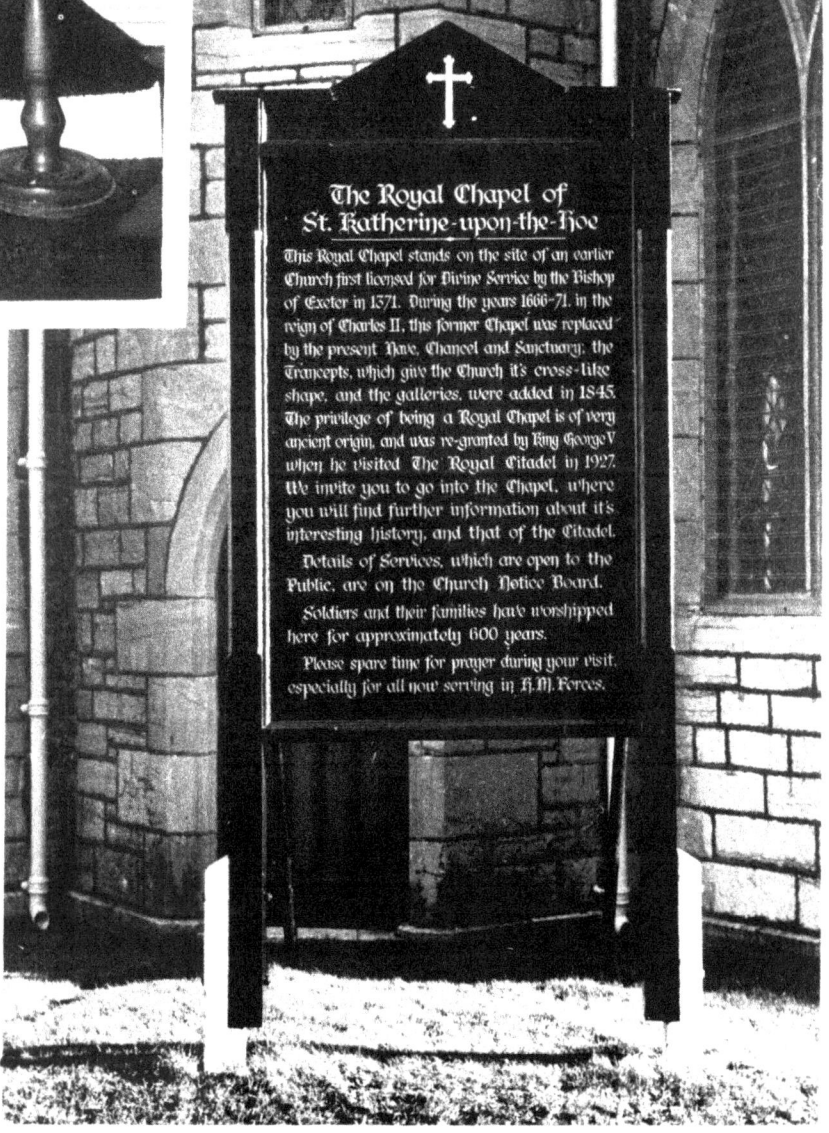

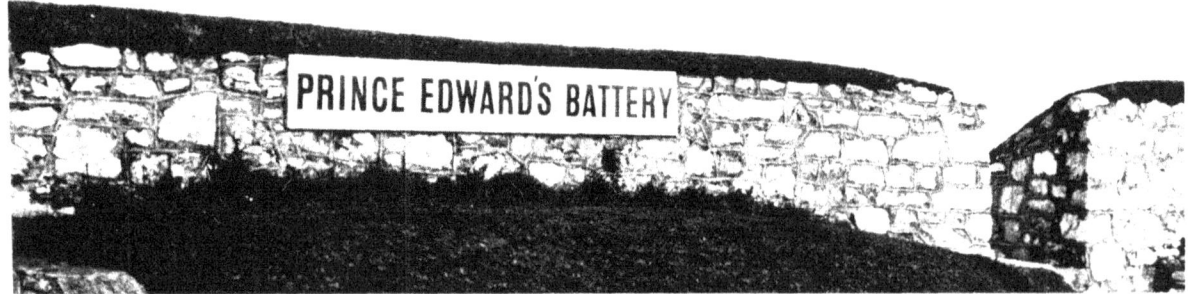

Bastions linked by Curtain Walls

Four sections of the extensive defending walls are grouped on this page. There were five bastions joined by curtain walls with saluting positions or batteries which made up the Citadel's main line of defence. They can be walked for most of their length and provide excellent views over the city, Hoe and Sound. Their height and size can best be appreciated from the road below the fortification on the seaward side. The saluting platforms are still used for special occasions using four guns kept in the citadel. The barrel of a gun made in Strasbourg in 1778 now stands on the Prince Henry's demi-bastion.

The Citadel's Cannon
These four sixty-four pounder cannon date from 1876 and now maintain silent duty from the high wall. They were last fired in 1906. A wide angle of firing is achieved by using the traversing carriage on the metal runners. The letters R.G.F. on them refer to the Royal Gun Factory at Woolwich where they were made.

Note, this content was originally on the front cover of the Citadel booklet, which is why there is space on this page.

The Main Gate

This very ornate entrance gate to the citadel was built by Sir Thomas Fitz in 1670 and is one of the finest examples of its kind in the country. It bears the Royal Arms and Cypher together with the Arms of John Grenville, Earl of Bath. The central niche originally held a statue of King Charles II. The old dry moat passed immediately in front of the entrance over which a drawbridge was worked by chains still in position in the archway.

Arthur L. Clamp – the man behind the books

Arthur Leslie Clamp was a man of boundless energy with a passion for helping others, particularly through his love of history. A printer by trade, he started his career in a printing company before moving his family from Exeter to Plymouth to teach at the Plymouth College of Art and Design, where he eventually became the Head of the Printing Department.

Arthur with his five children.

A Devoted Family Man

Despite his love of teaching, Arthur prioritised his family, always making it home by 5:30pm for tea. He and his wife, Rosemary, raised five children: Susan, Angela, Elizabeth, David, and Steven. Arthur would often combine his love of family and history by taking his children on Sunday walks, encouraging them to appreciate historical monuments by taking photos or making crayon rubbings of gravestones for his books. The family home at 203 Elburton Road was a hub of activity, with a large garden, featuring a two-storey fort and a makeshift swimming pool.

A Lifelong Learner and Adventurer

Arthur's thirst for knowledge extended beyond history to a deep curiosity about the world. He was passionate about exploring different cultures, traditions, and cuisines, often taking advantage of his long summer holidays as a teacher to travel to places like India, Russia, South America, the middle east and the USA, sometimes bringing one of his children along. This adventurous spirit even influenced his home life, as seen by the short-lived family tradition of steam-cooking vegetables after a trip to Iceland.

History is a prominent feature of family days out

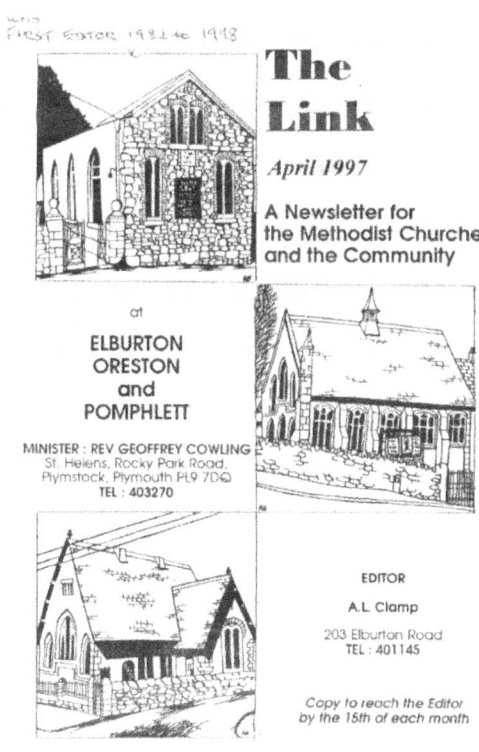

Community and Philanthropic Spirit

His commitment to serving others was evident in his long-standing involvement with the Elburton Methodist Church. He was the Sunday School Superintendent for over 15 years and served as the editor of the wider church's monthly newsletter, "The Link," for a similar duration. After Rosemary's very sad passing, Arthur later remarried and, following a chance encounter with a professor from India, established a connection with a missionary school in Chennai. Together with his new wife, Christine, he co-founded a "Sponsor a Child's Education" program that continues to this day.

Pictured left – The cover of 'The Link' complete with hand drawn sketches of each church by Angela
Below right – Arthur Clamp promoting his latest book
Below left – Arthur at home with his first wife, Rosemary
Below centre – Arthur on holiday with his second wife, Christine

A Legacy of Learning and Positivity

Arthur's greatest passion was history, which he brought to life through tireless research, documentation, and the many books he authored. He was driven by a need to "never be stuck in a rut," constantly seeking new experiences, meeting new people, and expanding his knowledge. With a positive attitude and a great sense of humour, he was always ready to help others, leaving a lasting impact on his family and community. His children, Susan, Angela, Elizabeth, David, and Steven, remember him with love and gratitude.

David Clamp, 2025

A Legacy of Local History

Below is the story of how Arthur L Clamp began writing books, in his own words, drafted shortly before he passed away in 2001. I have only made minor alterations to this text, correcting grammatical errors that he did not survive to correct himself. When I first discovered this text, I was shocked to see my name mentioned. It seems that, unbeknownst to me, I shared my first PC with him. I suspect he used it during the day when I was at school, although I do have one memory of sitting with him and showing him how it worked. It has been a pleasure to pick up where he left off and see his books republished and redistributed, and to know that I was part of the story, even back then. It was also fascinating to discover that his pricing structure matches the way I have tried to price the books, with a third going to local sellers and the rest covering printing costs with a little left over for my expenses.

I am his eldest grandson, and it is a privilege to curate his legacy, which we are calling 'The Clamp Collection'. The very last line of the text originally reads "The following pages list all the titles." Sadly, that page is missing and we have no record of all the books he published and knowing that some of those were researched by other authors makes the process of finding them even harder. I look forward to one day completing the collection and seeing them all available again. And maybe, one day, I'll even start writing my own to add to the series. For now, here is his story in his own words.

Steven Gibson, 2025

Writing and Publishing Booklets on Local Topics and Areas

I started this interest in either 1968 or 1969 when living in Woodford. I had by these dates established the Department of Printing and I think I must have been looking for something different to do. The first titles were of A5 size proofed from type set at Clarke, Doble and Brendon, Ltd., Plymouth printers, and then made up into pages and printed at Sawtell and Neilson, Ltd., Totnes.

Then began a slow process of getting them out to shops, etc. which proved to be more time consuming and difficult than actually researching, writing and getting the books into print. However, I persisted and opened a business account with Barclays Bank on the Broadway. I was advised to give it a title so I called it "Westway Publications". There came along another problem, one of storage of paper and finished books which was solved when the family moved to Elburton in 1970.

I changed the printer to Penwell, Ltd., Callington, Cornwall, as he was then just setting up himself and his prices seemed very reasonable. I did not get any of the printers to make up the complete books. I hand folded the flat printed sheets, stitched the books on a small manual table stitcher and trimmed them in a small hand turned guillotine which I bought from someone in Penzance for £40. It was brought up in a van.

The trouble and time going to and fro to Callington was too much so I transferred the printing to PDS Printers, Prince Rock, Plymouth, and I have been with them ever since. Now they are at Plympton which is easy to reach and they fold the flat sheets which was turning out to be a long chore which only saved a small part of the printing costs.

All my first titles were written by myself. I took the photographs and developed them in the loft of the house, the type was set by now on a computer situated in the house at Elburton from which I had collected photographic lengths of text to cut up and law down as pages.

At some point I decided that I would do my own film processing of lith film so I bought a large second hand process camera from Kingsbridge and learnt through trial and error to make line negatives of the text and halftone negatives of the illustrations which proved more difficult than I anticipated. The main problem was trying to keep the developer in the large dish at the correct temperature as any change would affect the developing time. I replaced this old camera with a brand new one bought from Croydon, Surrey, costing £900. This has turned out to be a great asset cutting out an expensive part of the printer's costs and one crucial aspect of the work which I could control.

By the middle 1970s there were many outlets I had contacted in Plymouth, up to Dartmoor, Exeter, around to Torbay, Totnes, Dartmouth and the South Hams. The market for local books was much greater than I had first thought and through getting to know many local people undertaking research themselves had the chance to help and make up books for other people who had in most instances, got together a collection of photographs with some text in a rather muddled way. Through my experience in print I was able to shape up their work and get it into print and in every case I had to pay the printer and let the person have the royalties. In the majority of titles produced in this manner this was another way of producing titles and it did give some profit to my work. However, I must say that in a few cases I lost out by either the other person getting the numbers wrong, not returning any monies from stock I delivered or they thought that more of their books should have been sold.

The print run was usually 1,000 copies and from time to time I have had reprints of 250 copies. It took about ten years to clear the first print run so I always had large stocks in the garage, workshop, etc. The numbers sold during the early years was about 7,000 copies a year increasing to around 9,000 copies and for the whole of the enterprise about 500,000 have been sold. The booklets have become part of the local scene and many people collect them, shops regularly order copies and I go around certain areas month by month restocking or replacing titles as necessary.

During the past year or so I have started setting the text on a Packard Bell PC, something which I should have done some years back. I share it with Steven Gibson, my grandson. There appears to be no end to the market for local books, but I could not earn a regular income because of the long time it takes to sell stock.

However, now exceeding 100 titles made up mainly of A4 twenty-four page booklets, some folded guides, with selling prices set with a third going to the shop which is the trade custom, the original idea has been quite successful and could go on for ever.

Apart from monetary benefits, however spasmodically these might be, I have learnt a lot myself, met many interesting people and have become part of the local scene with requests to give talks and to advise people about getting into print.

Arthur L Clamp, 2001

This newspaper article, published by the Evening Herald on 17th August 2001, forms a good record of his life. Just as he encourages us to learn more about local history, we encourage you to learn a little about him. For that reason, we have included these pages at the back of all the most recently republished books, in honour of his memory and recognition of his contribution to the community.

www.ingramcontent.com/pod-product-compliance
Lightning Source LLC
Chambersburg PA
CBHW061402070526
44584CB00031B/4145